Carly's Angels

Mary Ruth Weaver

AuthorHouse™
1663 Liberty Drive
Bloomington, IN 47403
www.authorhouse.com
Phone: 1 (800) 839-8640

© 2017 Mary Ruth Weaver. All rights reserved.

No part of this book may be reproduced, stored in a retrieval system,
or transmitted by any means without the written permission of the author.

Published by AuthorHouse 08/25/2017

ISBN: 978-1-5462-0636-1 (sc)
ISBN: 978-1-5462-0638-5 (hc)
ISBN: 978-1-5462-0637-8 (e)

Print information available on the last page.

Any people depicted in stock imagery provided by Thinkstock are models,
and such images are being used for illustrative purposes only.
Certain stock imagery © Thinkstock.

This book is printed on acid-free paper.

Because of the dynamic nature of the Internet, any web addresses or links contained in this book may have changed
since publication and may no longer be valid. The views expressed in this work are solely those of the author and do not
necessarily reflect the views of the publisher, and the publisher hereby disclaims any responsibility for them.

All scriptures taken from KJV

authorHOUSE®

In loving memory of Caitlin Marie Cantos
and Anna Catherine Pellegrino.

For Carly, Sandy, Marvin, and Lori,
with all my love.

She looked in her bedroom.
She looked under her bed.
She looked in her closet.
She looked under her toy box.
But Carly could not find them.

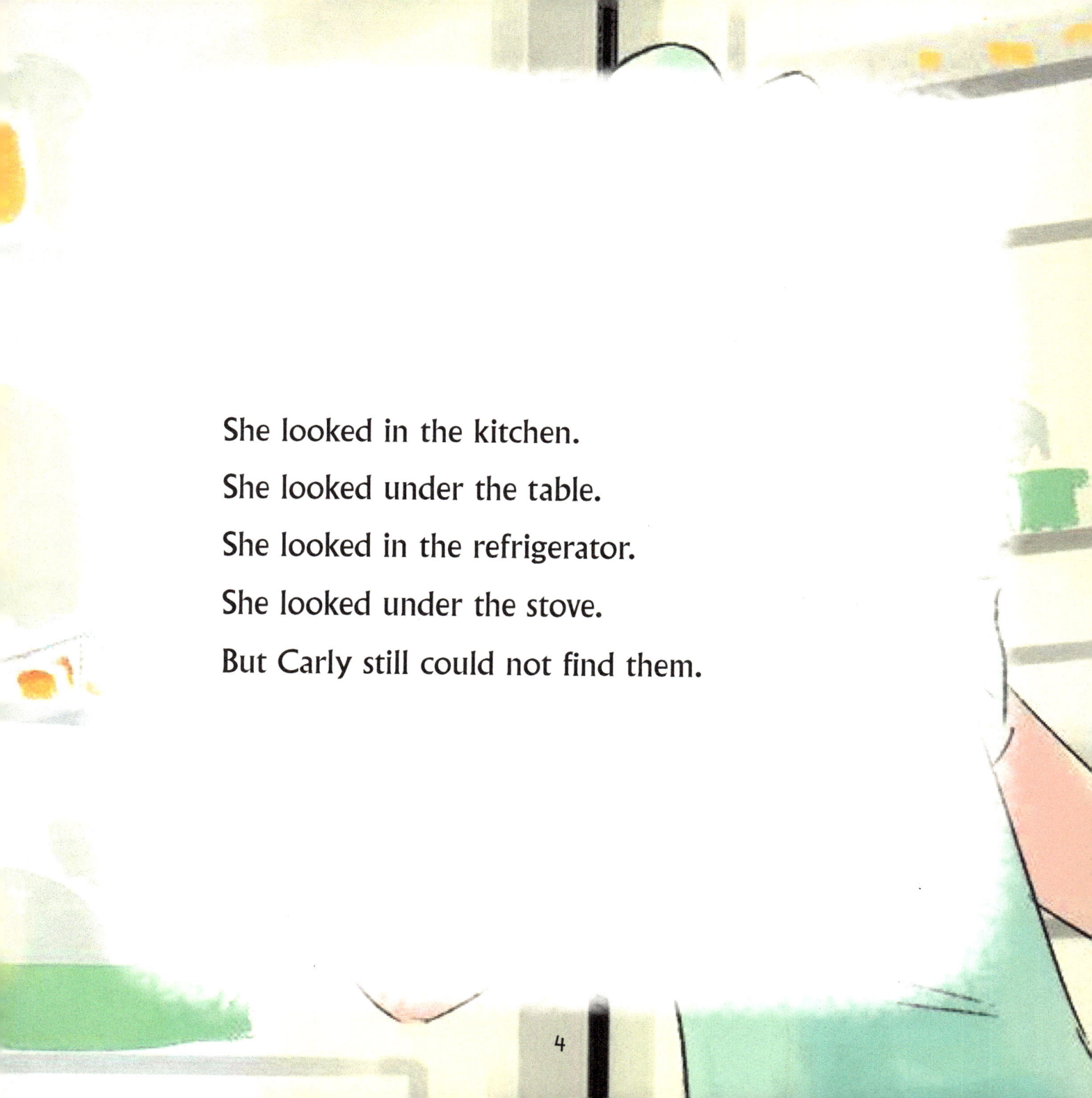

She looked in the kitchen.

She looked under the table.

She looked in the refrigerator.

She looked under the stove.

But Carly still could not find them.

She looked in the living room.

She looked under the sofa.

She looked in the cabinet.

She looked under the coffee table.

But, again, Carly could not find them.

Just then her mom asked, "Carly, what are you looking for?"

"My angels," replied Carly.

"Your what?" asked Mom.

"My angels, my angels," said Carly.

"Do you mean your little dolls with the fairy wings?" asked Mom.

"No, Mom, not my fairy dolls, my angels," answered Carly.

"Where did you hear about angels?" asked Mom.

"From you, Mom," answered Carly.

"From me?" asked Mom.

"Yes," said Carly. "I heard you talking to Grandma Lori on the phone. You said that I have angels watching over me, but I've looked everywhere, and I can't find them!"

Mom laughed. She picked up Carly and gave her a big hug. Then she sat her on her lap.

"Would you like to hear the story about your angels?" asked Mom.

"Yes!" shouted Carly. "Where are they?"

"Well, before you were born, Dad and I had a beautiful baby girl named Caitlin Marie. She was your sister," said Mom.

"My sister? Did she look like me?" asked Carly.

"Yes, she did," answered Mom. "She was just as pretty as you are."

"Well, where is she?" asked Carly.

"Right now, she's in heaven with God," said Mom.

"In heaven? When can I see her?" asked Carly.

"Someday, when God decides it's time for you to see her," said Mom.

"How long did she live with you and Dad?" asked Carly.

Mom answered, "She lived with us for four wonderful months."

"But why is she in heaven with God? Why isn't she here with us?" asked Carly.

"Sometimes God allows a person to live many, many years on this earth, like your great-grandma Katie. She lived eighty-two years, and then three days before you were born, she went to heaven to be with God," said Mom.

"And sometimes He lets a person live on this earth for a short time, like your sister Caitlin Marie."

Her mother continued on to say that they don't know why such things happen, but they do know that in the Holy Bible, God's Word says,

To every thing there is a season, and a time to every purpose under the heaven: a time to be born, and a time to die.

(Ecclesiastes 3:1–2, kjv)

Carly began to cry. "My sister is with God right now?"

"Yes," answered Mom.

"But you see, Carly, we all belong to God. He allows us to live on this earth for a time, and then He decides when to call us home to be with Him in heaven. While we're here, we are to love Him, worship Him, and let others know that His Son, Jesus Christ, is our Lord and Savior."

Mom said that the Holy Bible also says,

For he shall give his angels charge over

thee, to keep thee in all thy ways.

(Psalm 91:11, kjv)

Mom continued, "So when I told your Grandma Lori about the angels watching over you, I meant the angel God sent to watch over you the moment you were born. We call that angel a guardian angel. And because your sister and Great-grandma Katie went to heaven to be with God and his angels, we know that they are all watching over you. And do you know what your grandma Lori said when Great-grandma Katie went to heaven?"

"No, Mom, what did she say?" asked Carly.

"She said, 'God took Great-grandma Katie to heaven to babysit Caitlin Marie, and right now she's up there rocking her to sleep.'"

"She's a good great-grandma to take care of Caitlin, huh, Mom?" asked Carly.

"Yes, and even though you can't see them, their memories live within us so we won't ever forget them," said Mom.

"I love my sister Caitlin Marie and my greatgrandma Katie," said Carly.

"I do too," said Mom.

"Can we call Grandma Lori right now?" asked Carly.

"I suppose so," answered Mom. "But why?"

"Because I want to tell Grandma Lori I love her too!"

The End

Mary Ruth Weaver
Yuma, AZ
kidzboox@outlook.com

CPSIA information can be obtained
at www.ICGtesting.com
Printed in the USA
BVOW05*1749041017

496330BV00013B/48/P